Fact Finders®

PERSPECTIVES on HISTORY

BENEDICT ARNOLD

OR SELFISH TRAITOR?

BATTLEFIELD HERO

by Jessica Gunderson

Consultant:
Richard Bell
Associate Professor of History
University of Maryland, College Park

CAPSTONE PRESS
a capstone imprint

Fact Finders Books are published by Capstone Press,
1710 Roe Crest Drive, North Mankato, Minnesota 56003
www.capstonepub.com

Library of Congress Cataloging-in-Publication Data
Gunderson, Jessica.
Benedict Arnold : battlefield hero or selfish traitor? / by Jessica Gunderson.
pages cm. — (Fact finders. Perspectives on History)
Summary: "Describes Benedict Arnold's actions during the Revolutionary War and his betrayal
of the Patriot cause"— Provided by publisher.
Includes bibliographical references and index.
ISBN 978-1-4765-0243-4 (library binding)
ISBN 978-1-4765-3407-7 (paperback)
ISBN 978-1-4765-3415-2 (ebook PDF)
1. Arnold, Benedict, 1741–1801—Juvenile literature. 2. American loyalists—Biography—Juvenile
literature. 3. Generals—United States—Biography—Juvenile literature. 4. United States.
Continental Army—Biography—Juvenile literature. 5. United States—History—Revolution,
1775–1783—Juvenile literature. I. Title.
E278.A7G86 2014
973.382092—dc23
[B]   2013003358

Editorial Credits
Mari Bolte, editor; Ted Williams, designer; Svetlana Zhurkin, media researcher;
Laura Manthe, production specialist

Photo Credits
Getty Images: Time Life Pictures/Mansell, 25; Library of Congress, 8, 10, 13, 17, 26; Line of Battle
Enterprise, cover (middle right and bottom left), 21, 23; Newscom: Design Pics, 14; North Wind
Picture Archives, 5, 7, 19, 22; Shutterstock: Alena Hovorkova (design elements), throughout,
Dennis Donohue, cover (background), Dianka Pyzhova (design elements), throughout, exshutter
(vintage paper sheet), 7 and throughout, Oleksiy Fedorov (background texture), throughout;
Wikipedia: Americasroof, 29

Direct Quotes
p. 11 from *Benedict Arnold: Patriot and Traitor* by William Sterne Randall (New York: William
Morrow, 1990)
p. 24 from "Letter to the Inhabitants of America." Benedict Arnold. October 7, 1780. 1 April 2013.
(http://teachingamericanhistory.org/library/index.asp?document=885)
p. 27 from "Obituary of Benedict Arnold." *Columbian Centinel.* August 1, 1801. 1 April 2013.
(http://www.earlyamerica.com/earlyamerica/obits/arnold.html)
p. 29 from "Benedict Arnold: A Traitor, but Once a Patriot" by Linda L. Creighton. U.S. News.
June 27, 2008. 1 April 2013. (http://www.usnews.com/news/national/articles/2008/06/27/
benedict-arnold-a-traitor-but-once-a-patriot?page=2)

Printed and bound in China. 5174

TABLE OF CONTENTS

A Spy in the Night

The night of September 22, 1780, was still. Clouds blanketed the moon. American General Benedict Arnold peered through the trees, listening for the tiniest sound. Earlier, the nearby fort of West Point had bustled with soldiers, but now all was quiet. Would André come?

Then the general heard a crunch of leaves. A figure in a dark coat appeared. "Arnold," he said. "You have something for me?"

Arnold's hand shook as he reached into his pocket for the papers. He slipped them into British Major John André's outstretched palm. "Deliver to General Clinton," he whispered. He swallowed, gaining courage as he spoke. "This information will help the British capture West Point."

Benedict Arnold, the man who had led the Americans to victory in several battles, had just committed **treason**. What could lead a distinguished general to betray the **Patriot** cause?

treason: the crime of betraying your country

Patriot: a person who sided with the American colonies during the Revolutionary War

Benedict Arnold (right) gave important information to the British.

Chapter 1

FIERY PATRIOT

Benedict Arnold was born in 1741 in Norwich, Connecticut. His parents were wealthy merchants. However, in Benedict's teen years, his father began drinking heavily. His father's drinking led to the Arnolds losing their family fortune.

Arnold quit school to become a shop apprentice. He learned how to run a successful business. He later opened a drugstore in New Haven, Connecticut. He eventually bought three ships and launched a trading business. But British laws put heavy taxes on trade goods. Arnold fell into **debt**. He, and many other merchants, began **smuggling** goods to avoid paying the taxes.

In 1766 a crew member threatened to expose Arnold's smuggling. An angry Arnold rounded up a group of men. He stormed the man's home, dragged him out, and beat him. Arnold was arrested and fined for disturbing the peace.

debt: money that a person owes

smuggle: to bring something or someone into or out of a country illegally

Increasingly frustrated by British taxation, Arnold joined the Sons of Liberty. The secret group often used violence to oppose British laws. In 1774 Arnold organized a local **militia**.

Colonists met to protest British taxes.

militia: a group of citizens who are trained to fight, but who only serve in an emergency

FACT

Attacking a crew member wasn't Arnold's only outburst. While on a trading voyage in the West Indies, a British sea captain insulted Arnold's manners. Angered, Arnold challenged him to a duel. The captain was wounded in the duel. Fearing for his life, the captain apologized.

Frustration against British laws and taxes led to the Revolutionary War (1775–1783). Arnold was elected colonel of the New Haven militia. He gathered men and began marching toward the heart of the fight. When he reached Cambridge, Massachusetts, he learned the Patriots were in trouble. Weapons and ammunition were in short supply.

Arnold had traveled to Lake Champlain in New York on business trips. While there, he'd seen large amounts of ammunition stored at Fort Ticonderoga. He also knew the fort was only lightly guarded by the British. He suggested leading a raid on the fort.

Ethan Allen (center) received all the credit for the Ticonderoga attack in this famous painting.

FACT

The New Haven council did not want to oppose the British. They refused to give the militia weapons. Arnold threatened to break into the storehouse. The council finally gave in.

Arnold left his **troops** behind and traveled alone toward New York. His captains would **recruit** more troops, then rejoin Arnold.

When Arnold arrived in Vermont, he had a surprise. Another colonel, Ethan Allen, was also planning a raid on Ticonderoga. If Arnold wanted a part of the attack, he would have to share leadership with Allen. Arnold reluctantly agreed.

The two colonels captured the fort on May 10. After the victory Allen's men, the Green Mountain Boys, celebrated by looting the fort. Arnold demanded that they stop. Allen refused. Some drunken Green Mountain Boys even took shots at Arnold.

Later that month Arnold's troops finally arrived. He led a successful attack on the British warship *George*. He also took the British outpost of St. Johns. When Allen left, Arnold expected to take command of the fort. But Congress gave the fort to Colonel Benjamin Hinman, a man with many friends in politics. An upset Arnold left Ticonderoga.

troop: a group of soldiers

recruit: to ask someone to join a company or organization

The march to Quebec took Arnold's troops through the Maine wilderness.

Arnold was not about to give up on his country. He proposed an attack on the British-controlled Canadian cities of Quebec and Montreal. General George Washington liked Arnold's idea. He placed Arnold in charge of attacking Quebec.

In September 1775 Arnold led 1,000 men through Maine. Freezing rain and snow slowed them down. The march took twice as long as planned. Food supplies ran low. Although tired and weak, Arnold remained a confident leader. He was often seen riding ahead of his troops to make a path through the snow.

Finally, after six weeks, the troops reached Quebec. They attacked during a New Year's Eve blizzard. Arnold was shot in his left leg. Two-thirds of Arnold's troops were killed or captured.

Despite the loss, the injured Arnold refused to retreat. He and his small army laid siege to Quebec for months. The newly-promoted Brigadier General Arnold used his own money to feed and supply the troops. As the winter wore on, he lost more soldiers to illness. When the spring thaw came, the British sent 15,000 men to Quebec. Arnold's army was forced to retreat.

DURING THE SIEGE, ARNOLD WROTE:

"I have no thoughts of leaving this proud town until I first enter it in triumph ... I know no fear."

retreat: to move back or withdraw from a difficult situation

siege: an attack designed to surround a place and cut it off from supplies or help

Chapter 2

QUARRELS AND DISAPPOINTMENTS

Arnold had several arguments with Colonel Moses Hazen during the events at Ticonderoga and Quebec. Hazen was a Patriot commander who lived in Quebec. During the army's retreat from the city, Arnold ordered that supplies should be taken along. Hazen recognized the supplies as goods taken from shopkeepers he knew. He refused to help Arnold. In the end, most of the supplies were lost or stolen.

Both men accused the other of stealing military goods. Then Hazen blamed Arnold for the defeat at Quebec. Their fights eventually led to a hearing in the summer of 1776. Arnold was angry about being mistrusted. Congress dismissed the charges, but Arnold would never forget this insult.

In October 1776 Arnold positioned warships on the Hudson River. His action stalled the British advance on Lake Champlain. However, the colonists were outnumbered and Arnold realized that defeat was near.

Arnold commanded the American ships to escape. When it looked as if all was lost, he set fire to the ships to prevent the British from taking them.

Some members of Congress questioned Arnold's actions. General William Maxwell blamed Arnold for destroying the fleet. Congress also kept questioning his expenses. Arnold began to feel as though his own government was against him. He had no strong ally in Congress to speak for him. He felt he was passed over for promotions he deserved.

Arnold resigned from duty several times but always returned to military service.

Arnold in 1776

FACT
George Washington personally asked Arnold to return to the military in 1777.

Arnold's battlefield victories showed off his ability as a military leader. But his temper made him few friends. He quarreled fiercely with any who disagreed with his ideas. General George Washington had faith in Arnold's abilities. After a victory in April 1777, Arnold was finally named major general.

Arnold set himself apart as a military hero during the Battle of Saratoga.

In late 1777 word spread that the British were approaching Saratoga, New York. Arnold's superior, General Horatio Gates, wanted to fight from behind the fort's walls. Arnold thought the colonists should march out and attack. Gates disliked Arnold's constant complaining. He did everything he could to get Arnold to resign. He stopped inviting Arnold to officers' meetings. He also began reassigning Arnold's soldiers.

On September 19 Arnold led 2,000 troops into a fierce battle. He sent messages to Gates to send reinforcements. But Gates refused. Without help Arnold's men had to return to the fort.

On October 7, 1777, another battle broke out. Gates told Arnold to stay in his tent. Arnold ignored him and charged into battle. When the soldiers saw him, they cheered. Spirited by Arnold's presence, the American forces killed or captured more than 600 British soldiers. During the fighting Arnold was shot in the leg. His horse fell on top of him, shattering the same leg.

The British retreated. Ten days later, they surrendered. The victory was a turning point in the war. It helped the colonists believe they could win. It also convinced France to aid the colonists. Without Arnold, the battle may not have been won. But Gates sent reports to Congress that didn't mention Arnold. Congress awarded Gates a medal. Arnold got nothing.

Chapter 3

A CHANGED MIND

Arnold spent the next five months recovering from his wounds. During this time, the **Continental Congress** voted to promote Arnold. But the promotion came too late. Arnold had doubts about the new American government. He felt he hadn't gotten the respect he deserved.

He was also frustrated with Congress. He felt Congress members played favorites, promoting friends instead of proven leaders. To Arnold, Congress behaved as unfairly as the British government.

General Washington still believed in Arnold. He appointed Arnold military commander of Philadelphia. Congress met in Philadelphia. Arnold was now surrounded by people he didn't trust. But his high rank meant that he no longer had to win their support. Instead, he spoke out against harsh punishments issued to British supporters known as Loyalists. He also made his thoughts about Congress known.

the Arnold mansion in Philadelphia

Away from the battlefield, Arnold sought wealth and power. He made friends with wealthy Loyalists. He threw huge parties, traveled in fancy carriages, and bought a grand home. However, his military salary couldn't support his new lifestyle. He began using his position of power to make suspicious business deals. He began to struggle with debt.

Continental Congress: leaders from the 13 original American Colonies who made up the American government from 1774 to 1789

Arnold's attitude and rich lifestyle angered many Patriots. In February 1779 Joseph Reed filed charges against him. Reed was a lawyer, a member of Congress, and a former military man. Reed believed Arnold had abused his power. A lengthy trial began. Arnold was confident the charges would be dropped. He felt he'd done nothing wrong.

Meanwhile, Arnold married Peggy Shippen, the daughter of a Loyalist. She had many friends in the British army. Through her friends, Arnold heard that the British were offering **bribes** to colonial officers willing to change sides.

REED'S LIST OF CHARGES AGAINST BENEDICT ARNOLD

√ granting illegal passes to Loyalist ships

√ closing shops in order to buy foreign goods

√ mistreating militiamen

√ illegally buying a ship

√ using public wagons for private use

√ helping a Loyalist travel to British lines

√ refusing to explain his use of public wagons

√ neglecting Patriots and meeting with Loyalists

Desperate for money and losing faith in the Patriot cause, Arnold considered the idea. If caught helping the British, he could be put to death. But if successful, he would be richly rewarded. He also believed that the Patriot cause was lost. He wanted to be on the winning side.

bribe: money or gifts used to persuade someone to do something, especially something illegal or dishonest

Chapter 4

TURNED TRAITOR

In May 1779 Arnold contacted British Major John André. He said he would help the British—for a price. The British worked with Arnold for months to reach an agreement.

Meanwhile, Arnold was found guilty of using his military position for personal gain. To make matters worse, George Washington, his former supporter, issued a public **reprimand** about Arnold's behavior. Arnold felt humiliated. He firmly made up his mind to aid the British.

SECRET NAMES

Arnold and André used code names to communicate. Arnold named himself "Monk" or "Gustavus." André's code names were "John Anderson" and "Lothario." Messages were written with a three-number code with *Bailey's Dictionary* as the key. The first number was the page number the word was found on. The second number gave the line. The third number was the word.

André told Arnold that British General Henry Clinton wanted to capture West Point, a key site in New York. Clinton would need information on West Point. He also wanted to capture the fort's 3,000 troops. For this betrayal, Arnold would earn 20,000 pounds, nearly $5 million today. Arnold agreed.

Arnold asked George Washington for command of West Point. Washington gave it to him.

reprimand: a severe and formal criticism

Arnold (left) and André met in secret.

Once Arnold had settled in at West Point, he arranged a secret meeting with André. The meeting took place on September 22, 1780. André sailed to a place near West Point on the British warship *Vulture*. Arnold gave André the layout of West Point. He also shared General Washington's location. Capturing the general would be a great victory for the British.

REDRAWING HISTORY

There are many ways an artist can redraw history. A battle can be shown as a victory or a loss. A man can be shown as a hero or a villain. Compare these two works showing Benedict Arnold. What do they tell you about the popular opinion of Benedict Arnold during the time they were painted?

WOODCUT

This woodcut was done in 1780. It shows Arnold fleeing for his life after being discovered as a traitor. He is alone and looking over his shoulder for anyone chasing him.

During the meeting two American cannon crews fired upon the *Vulture*. The ship fled. André had lost his getaway ship. He would have to escape on foot.

Arnold wrote some passes to help André travel safely. André was stopped and searched by colonial troops. The troops, not satisfied with the passes, searched André. They found the West Point papers in his boot.

THE BATTLE OF SARATOGA
by Alonzo Chappel

This engraving was made in 1858. It shows Arnold's horse falling on his leg during the Battle of Saratoga in 1777. Arnold's troops press forward bravely while their enemies run away.

Arnold received news of André's capture on September 25. He knew he would soon be exposed as a traitor. He found the *Vulture* and escaped to safety. André was not so lucky. He was found guilty of **espionage** and hanged.

ARNOLD IN THE NEWS

Arnold wrote a letter to the American people called "Letter to the Inhabitants of America." It was published in a Loyalist newspaper. In his letter, he explained his actions. He said that Congress was wrong. Being ruled by Great Britain was the only way to solve the country's problems. He wrote, "The reunion of the British Empire [is] the best and only means to dry up the streams of misery that have deluged this country."

A Philadelphia newspaper had a different take on Arnold's actions. They printed a picture of Arnold riding in a parade wagon. Arnold was shown with two faces and holding a letter to the devil.

espionage: the actions of a spy to gain sensitive national, political, or economic information

General Washington was shocked when he heard
of Arnold's betrayal. He had trusted and stood up for
the general. As word of Arnold's acts spread across the
colonies, Patriots showed their rage. They burned figures
of Arnold. A mob destroyed the graves of his father and
brother. Congress ordered that Arnold's name be erased
from military records.

Benedict Arnold
escaped aboard
the *Vulture*.

Arnold went to New York City. He often met with British officials. He told them everything he knew about American troops and strategies. He was made a brigadier general in the British Army. Clinton did not trust him. Eventually though, Arnold was allowed to lead several attacks.

In October 1781 British General Charles Cornwallis surrendered. Arnold traveled to London to ask the King to continue the war. But at that point, the war was over. The Patriots had won independence.

the surrender of General Cornwallis at Yorktown, Virginia

After the war Arnold made various requests for positions in the British government. He was never hired. Still struggling with debt, he begged the British government to pay him. He was given only a fraction of the promised amount because his plot had failed. Later he asked for money to replace property left behind in America. Many British people thought he was money hungry and would do anything to get paid.

After the war many Loyalists fled to Canada. Arnold decided to move his family there as well. He began a successful merchant business and often loaned money to other Loyalists. But some could not repay him and grew angry when he tried to collect the money. One night a crowd of Loyalists gathered outside his home, shouting "Traitor!" Even those who shared his views hated him for his betrayal.

Arnold moved to London. He tried to join in the British war against France, but his offer was again rejected. He died on June 14, 1801. His passing went unnoticed by most. The *Columbian Centinel* simply stated, "Died—In England, Brigadier-General Benedict Arnold; notorious throughout the world."

Chapter 5

ARNOLD'S LEGACY

Benedict Arnold has been remembered as America's most famous traitor. In the century following the Revolutionary War, historians painted Arnold as a corrupt, greedy, and dishonest traitor. His contributions to the success of the Revolution were overlooked. Some even suggested that he planned to betray America all along.

REMEMBERING BENEDICT ARNOLD

Several monuments in the United States recognize Arnold's heroic actions. But because of his betrayal, they do not name him. The Boot Monument in Saratoga National Park sits on the spot where Arnold was shot in the leg. The Battle of Saratoga Victory Monument has statues of three generals. The spot meant for Benedict Arnold stands empty.

In recent years historians have seen Arnold's key role in the Revolution. Without his early leadership, Americans may have lost the war. Recent biographer James Kirby Martin said, "The tragedy of Benedict Arnold is that his incredible acts … have been washed away and basically forgotten."

Benedict Arnold has been remembered as both a hero and a villain. What do you think?

FACT

The Boot Monument says, "In memory of the 'most brilliant soldier.'" The soldier is Arnold, but the monument does not mention his name.

GLOSSARY

bribe (BRIBE)—money or gifts used to persuade someone to do something, especially something illegal or dishonest

Continental Congress (kahn-tuh-nen-tuhl KAHNG-gruhs)—leaders from the 13 original American Colonies who made up the American government from 1774 to 1789

debt (DET)—money that a person owes

espionage (ESS-pee-uh-nahzh)—the actions of a spy to gain sensitive national, political, or economic information

militia (muh-LISH-uh)—a group of citizens who are trained to fight, but who only serve in an emergency

Patriot (PAY-tree-uht)—a person who sided with the American colonies during the Revolutionary War

recruit (ri-KROOT)—to ask someone to join a company or organization

reprimand (REP-ri-mand)—a severe and formal criticism

retreat (ri-TREET)—to move back or withdraw from a difficult situation

siege (SEEJ)—an attack designed to surround a place and cut it off from supplies or help

smuggle (SMUHG-uhl)—to bring something or someone into or out of a country illegally

treason (TREE-zuhn)—the crime of betraying your country

troop (TROOP)—a group of soldiers

READ MORE

Catel, Patrick. *Key People of the Revolutionary War.* Why We Fought: The Revolutionary War. Chicago: Heinemann Library, 2011.

Perritano, John. *The Causes of the American Revolution.* Understanding the American Revolution. New York: Crabtree Publishing Company, 2013.

Scarbrough, Mary Hertz. *Heroes of the American Revolution.* The Story of the American Revolution. North Mankato, Minn.: Capstone Press, 2013.

INTERNET SITES

FactHound offers a safe, fun way to find Internet sites related to this book. All of the sites on FactHound have been researched by our staff.

Here's all you do:
Visit *www.facthound.com*
Type in this code: 9781476502434

 Check out projects, games and lots more at **www.capstonekids.com**

CRITICAL THINKING USING THE COMMON CORE

1. Arnold began his career as an enthusiastic Patriot soldier. Do you think he was justified when he later changed sides? Use evidence from the text to support your answer. (Key Ideas and Details)

2. Examine the two paintings on pages 22–23. Compare and contrast them. How do these paintings impact viewers' perceptions of Benedict Arnold? Which painting do you think is more accurate? (Craft and Structure)

3. On page 29 the author states that, without Arnold's leadership, the Americans may have lost the war. Suppose that Arnold had fought for the British from the beginning of the war. How might the outcome of the war have been different? (Integration of Knowledge and Ideas)

INDEX